a gift for

from

OTHER GIFTBOOKS BY HELEN EXLEY:

Go Girl!
Looking for Mr Right
Battle of the Sexes
Men! by women
Birthday Girl
The Naughty Ladies' Book

OTHER BOOKS IN THIS SERIES:

A Woman's Work is Never Done
Too Soon for a Mid-Life Crisis
When I'm good I'm very very good – but when I'm bad
I'm better

Published simultaneously in 2007 by Helen Exley Giftbooks in Great Britain and
Helen Exley Giftbooks LLC in the USA.

12 11 10 9 8 7 6 5 4 3 2 1

Design, selection and arrangement copyright © 2007 Helen Exley
Cartoons copyright © 2007 Rowan Barnes-Murphy
The moral right of the authors has been asserted.
ISBN: 978-1-905130-37-5

Acknowledgements: The publishers are grateful for permission to reproduce copyright
material. Whilst every effort has been made to trace copyright holders, we would be
pleased to hear from any not here acknowledged. LYNDA BARRY: Copyright ©
Lynda Barry, used courtesy of Darhansoff, Verrill, Feldman Literary Agents, New
York, NY. ANGELA DOUGLAS: Reproduced from *Sounding Board*, *She Magazine*,
June 1985, by kind permission of Curtis Brown Group Ltd. HELEN FIELDING:
Reproduced from *Bridget Jones's Diary* by Helen Fielding, by kind permission of Pan
Macmillan. Copyright © Helen Fielding, 1996. KATHY LETTE: Reproduced from
Altar Ego by Kathy Lette, by kind permission of Pan Macmillan. Copyright © Kathy
Lette, 1998. ELIZABETH VON ARMIN: Reproduced from *Elizabeth And Her
German Garden* by Elizabeth von Armin by kind permission of Virago Press. JOYCE
GRENFELL: From *Turn Back The Clock: Her Best Songs And Monologues* by Joyce
Grenfell, Hodder & Stoughton, 1998. DOROTHY PARKER: The author wishes to
thank the National Association for the Advancement of Colored People for authorizing
the use of Dorothy Parker's work.
Helen Exley Giftbooks, 16 Chalk Hill, Watford, Herts, WD19 4BG, UK.
www.helenexleygiftbooks.com

GiRL TALK!

A HELEN EXLEY GIFTBOOK

ROWAN BARNES-MURPHY

"Women will talk to women anywhere, anytime. Old friends slight acquaintances. Total strangers. Bus queues. Underground trains. Grocer shops. It's the mechanism by which the world spins."

PETER GRAY, B.1928

"A night out with the girls
~ a marauding army that no father,
no boy, no man, no world
leader can stand against."

PAM BROWN, B.1928

"OUR PHONE BILL
IS EQUIVALENT TO THE
NATIONAL DEBT
OF VANUATU."

ISABEL WOLFF

The telephone has been the greatest boon granted to women – they are what keep the companies solvent.

PETER GRAY, B. 1928

Girls together don't need a reason to giggle themselves into near hysteria. Anything will do.

PAM BROWN, B.1928

"Everyone needs a friend with whom they can be splendidly, outrageously, silly."

"EVERY good thing
is better if you can
share it with a friend."

PAM BROWN, B.1928

Laugh and the world
laughs with you.
Cry and you cry with
your girlfriends.

LAURIE KUSLANSKY

Friends are there....
When your hopes are churned
and your nerves are knotted.
Talking about nothing in particular,
you can feel the tangles untwist.

CHARLOTTE GRAY, B.1937

There can be something
ever-so-slightly pleasurable about
confiding a broken heart
to a girl friend.

CLAIRE NEILSON

"FRIENDS PUT THE ENTIRE
WORLD TO RIGHTS OVER A CUP
OF TEA AND A BUN."

CHARLOTTE GRAY. B.1937

Being a woman is worse than being a farmer – there is so much harvesting and crop spraying to be done: legs to be waxed, underarms shaved, eyebrows plucked, feet pumiced, skin exfoliated and moisturized, spots cleansed, roots dyed, eyelashes tinted, nails filed, cellulite massaged, stomach muscles exercised. The whole performance is so highly tuned you only need to neglect it for a few days for the whole thing to go to seed.

HELEN FIELDING, FROM "BRIDGET JONES'S DIARY"

Women, all women,
worry about three things only.
Bad Hair days.
Shoe Shopping.
And Thinner Thighs.

KATHY LETTE, B.1958, FROM "ALTAR EGO"

The basic Female Body comes with the following accessories: garter belt, panti-girdle, crinoline, camisole, bustle, brassiere, stomacher, chemise, virgin zone, spike heels, nose ring, veil, kid gloves, fishnet stockings, fichu, bandeau, Merry Widow, weepers, chokers, barrettes, bangles, beads, lorgnette, feather boa, basic black, compact, Lycra stretch one-piece with modesty panel, designer peignoir, flannel nightie, lace teddy, bed, head.

MARGARET ATWOOD, B.1939

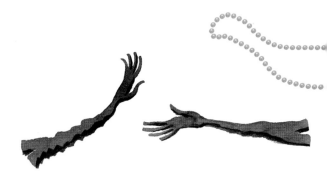

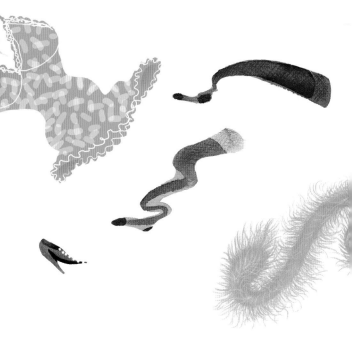

Women want men, careers, money,
children, friends, luxury, comfort,
independence, freedom, respect, love and a
three-dollar pantihose that won't run.

PHYLLIS DILLER, B.1917

WE POOR WOMEN

These are very confusing times. For the first time in history a woman is expected to combine intelligence with a sharp hairdo, a raised consciousness with high heels, and an open, non-sexist relationship with a tan guy who has a great bod.

LYNDA BARRY

We have no faith in ourselves. I have never met a woman who, deep down in her core, really believes she has great legs. And if she suspects that she might have great legs, then she's convinced that she has a shrill voice and no neck.

CYNTHIA HEIMEL, B.1947

"Mirror, Mirror,
on the Wall,
I don't want
to Hear
one Word
out of you."

Jean Kerr, b.1923

Diet Days

Eat drink and be merry,
for tomorrow we diet.

ALICE THOMAS ELLIS, B.1932

I used to fear that ice-cream would be the
ruin of me, but I gave up giving it up a
long time ago.

BEATRICE LILLIE (1898-1989)

Never eat anything at one sitting
that you can't lift.

MISS PIGGY

Life is so much harder when cheesecake
isn't the solution.

JENNY ECLAIR

SHOPPING SPREES

A good friend is the only
possible company on
a dress shopping expedition.

PAM BROWN, B.1928

And I always seem to think that the most delightful part of a shopping tour is to frequently change your mind.

ANITA LOOS (1893-1981)

"Diamonds are
a girl's best friend."
Leo Robin (1900~1984)
From "Gentlemen Prefer Blondes"

A woman can't be too rich,
too thin, or have too many
silk blouses.

JOYCE JILLSON

Whoever said money can't buy
happiness simply didn't know where
to go shopping.

BO DEREK, B.1956

"YOU'D BE SURPRISED
HOW MUCH IT COSTS
TO LOOK THIS CHEAP."

DOLLY PARTON, B.1946

"If you haven't got
anything nice to say
about anybody,
come sit next to me."

ALICE ROOSEVELT LONGWORTH (1884~1980)

I hate to spread rumours – but what else can one do with them?

AMANDA LEAR

Don't forget to tell everyone it's a secret.

GERALD F. LIEBERMAN

GOSSIP

Gossip is news
running ahead of itself
in a red satin dress.

LIZ SMITH

The idea of strictly
minding your own business
is mouldy rubbish.
Who could be so selfish?

MYRTLIE BARKER, B.1910

I believe all literature
started as gossip.

RITA MAE BROWN, B.1944

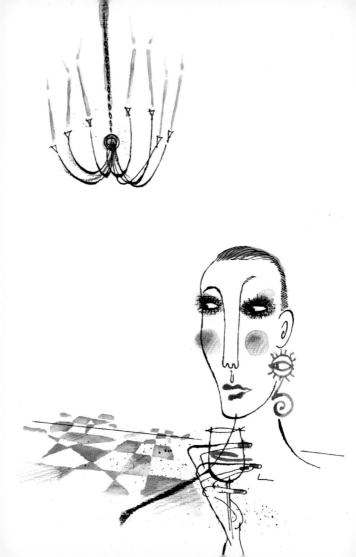

"A woman's tongue
is a deadly weapon
and the most difficult
thing in the world to
keep in order,
and things slip off
it with a facility
nothing short of
appalling."

ELIZABETH VON ARNIM (1866~1941)

Fighting is essentially a masculine idea; a woman's weapon is her tongue.

HERMIONE GINGOLD (1897-1987)

We continue to see one another
like two people that are resolved
to hate with civility.

LADY MARY WORTLEY MONTAGU (1689-1762),
ON THE DUCHESS OF MARLBOROUGH

Lack of education is an
extraordinary handicap when
one is being offensive.

JOSEPHINE TEY

Knowledge is power,
if you know it about the right person.

ETHEL WATTS MUMFORD (1878-1940)

Danger! It's your Friend!

Nothing is more dangerous than a friend
without discretion; even a prudent enemy
is preferable.

JEAN DE LA FONTAINE (1621-1695)

Never exaggerate your faults;
your friends will attend to that.

CICERO (106-43 B.C.)

To have a good enemy, choose a friend;
they know where to strike.

DIANE DE POITIERS (1499-1566)

iNSULTS!

Her face looks as if it had
worn out bodies.

NEW ENGLAND SAYING

At least, she is not any worse-looking than
she used to be in her youth;
hers are features which never alter,
unfortunately for her.

GEORGE SAND [AMANDINE AURORE LUCIE DUPIN]
(1804-1876)

There is nothing like the sight of an old
enemy down on their luck.

EURIPIDES (C.480-406 B.C.)

"She looks like she combs her hair with an egg~beater."

HEDDA HOPPER (1890~1966)

"THERE WAS NOTHING
WRONG WITH HER
THAT A VASECTOMY OF THE
VOCAL CHORDS WOULDN'T FIX."

LISA ALTHER, B.1944

If food did not exist it would be
well-nigh impossible to get certain types
off the phone, as one would be unable to
say, "Look, I've got to run but let's have
dinner sometime soon".

FRAN LEBOWITZ, B.1951

Dying's not so bad. At least I won't
have to answer the telephone.

RITA MAE BROWN, B.1944

WOMEN ~ AND OUR MEN

Women are natural guerillas.
Scheming, we nestle in the enemy's bed,
avoiding open warfare, watching the
options, playing the odds.

SALLY KEMPTON, B.1943

I came very late
to the women's mafia,
which is our answer
to the old boys' network.
Theirs starts at school;
we have to build
ours subsequently.

JEAN DENTON

"God gave women
intuition and femininity.
Used properly,
that combination
easily jumbles
the brain of
any man
I've ever met."

FARRAH FAWCETT. B.1948

A lady is one who never shows her underwear unintentionally.

LILLIAN DAY

A dress has no meaning unless it makes a man want to take it off.

FRANCOISE SAGAN, B.1935

Sex appeal is fifty per cent what you've got, and fifty per cent what people think you've got.

SOPHIA LOREN, B.1934

"A smart girl is one who knows how to play tennis, golf, piano... and dumb."

MARILYN MONROE (1926~1962)

The feminine faculty of anticipating or inventing what can and will happen is acute, and almost unknown to men.

COLETTE [SIDONIE-GABRIELLE] (1873-1954)

The real art of conversation is not only to say the right thing in the right place but to leave unsaid the wrong thing at the tempting moment.

DOROTHY NEVILL (1826-1913)

Women like the
simple things of life –
like men.

AUTHOR UNKNOWN

I love men, even though they are lying,
cheating scumbags.

GWYNETH PALTROW, B.1972

We love them and we hate them!
But it would be rather boring
without them!

EVELLN KLOSE

A wealthy, older man is like a little black
dress. It may fray a little around the edges,
but it never goes out of style.

RITA RUDNER, B.1956, FROM "TICKLED PINK"

Beauty
Before Brains

Any girl can be glamorous.
All you have to do
is stand still and look stupid.

HEDY LAMARR

The average girl would rather have beauty
than brains because she knows that the
average man can see much better than
he can think.

LADIES' HOME JOURNAL, 1947

Sexy Ladies

Your dresses should be tight
enough to show you're woman
and loose enough to show
you're a lady.

EDITH HEAD, ATTRIBUTED

Seamed stockings aren't subtle but they
certainly do the job.... If you really want
your guy paralytic with lust, stop
frequently to adjust the seams.

CYNTHIA HEIMEL, B.1947

On being asked where to wear perfume:
"Wherever one wants to be kissed".

COCO CHANEL (1883-1971),

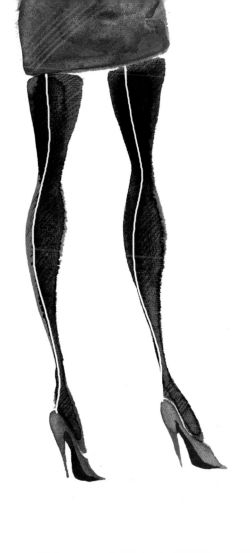

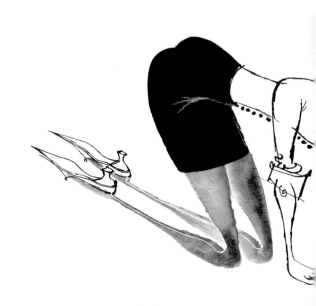

"Women speak because they wish to speak, whereas a man speaks only when driven to speech by something outside himself like, for instance, he can't find any clean socks."

Jean Kerr, b.1923

"My wife has a slight impediment in her speech. Every now and then she stops to breathe."

JIMMY DURANTE

"Once I didn't talk to my wife for six months", said the comedian.
"I didn't want to interrupt".

AUTHOR UNKNOWN

It has been said in the praise of some men, that they could talk whole hours upon anything; but it must be owned to the honour of the other sex, that there are many among them who can talk whole hours upon nothing.

JOSEPH ADDISON (1672-1719)

Nothing is dearer to a woman that a nice long obstetrical chat.

CORNELIA OTIS SKINNER
(1901–1979)

HYPOCHONDRIA

Mrs Ford kept a convenient little fund of
misery on hand, which she could draw
upon at the shortest notice... she was a
woman full of anxieties who liked to have
one within reach.

MARGARET OLIPHANT (1828-1897)

Only a friend can share with you
the sheer black comedy
of medical conditions.

PAM BROWN, B.1928

Lady Honiton was about the most
odious hypochondriac going, in a
perpetual state of unremitting battle with
the whole outer world in general, and
allapathists, homeopathists, and
hydropathists, in especial.

OUIDA (1839-1908)

From birth to age eighteen,
a girl needs good parents;
from eighteen to thirty-six
she needs good looks;
from thirty-five to fifty-five
she needs a good personality;
and from fifty-five on
she needs cash.

SOPHIE TUCKER (1884-1966)

FRiEND TaLk, GiRL TaLk

What is a friend to me?
In the simplest terms, it's someone
who will allow me to be the
way I am and not think me
totally round the bend.
Someone who can tell
by the look on my face
when I need to talk about
what's happening, or
not happening, in my life.
Someone who provides
non-judgmental support.

ANGELA DOUGLAS

Silences make the real conversations between friends. Not the saying but the never needing to say is what counts.

MARGARET LEE RUNBECK

"As one slowly
deteriorates it is very
comforting to have a
friend who is falling
apart at the
same speed."

PAM BROWN, B.1928

What a wretched lot of old shrivelled
creatures we shall be by-and-by.
Never mind – the uglier we get
in the eyes of others, the lovelier
we shall be to each other.

GEORGE ELIOT [MARY ANN EVANS] (1819-1880)

Yak~yak, Talk
Talk, Giggle

...we share laughter, scorn, music,
make-up, hair-dos, ambition
and dreams.

CLAIRE NEILSON

Girl talk is much the same in every age.
Appearance, men, ambitions and
despondencies. Boasting of conquests.
Dramatizing the dull. Speculating.
And bursts of giggling – helpless laughter
at the lunacies of life. The happy silliness
that keeps the dark at bay.

MARION C. GARRETTY (1917-2005)

HELEN EXLEY

Helen is known for her thoughtful,
sometimes serious, giftbooks about
families, mothers, daughters, love,
wisdom and trust. But she also
creates lighter, humorous titles.
She says, of *Girl Talk!*, "I immensely
enjoyed working with all the
ridiculous quips, insults and
Rowan's superb drawings.
It was great fun."

Helen Exley's books now sell in
over seventy countries and in many
languages on bookstalls as far apart
as Mumbai and Cape Town, Sydney
and San Francisco.

Rowan Barnes-Murphy

Rowan Barnes-Murphy's cartoons are
wicked, spiky and frayed at the edges.

His fantastically well-observed
characters are hugely popular
and have been used to advertise a
diverse range of products such
as cars, clothes and phones,
supermarkets, bank accounts
and greeting cards.

For more information contact:
**Helen Exley Giftbooks, 16 Chalk Hill,
Watford, Herts. WD19 4BG, UK.**

Helen Exley giftbooks are all on our website.
Have a look… maybe you will find many more
intriguing gift ideas!
www.helenexleygiftbooks.com